J. Merritte. Driver

Bible Temperance Hymns

A Choice Collection of Songs Adapted to the Present Phase of the....

J. Merritte. Driver

Bible Temperance Hymns
A Choice Collection of Songs Adapted to the Present Phase of the....

ISBN/EAN: 9783337083557

Printed in Europe, USA, Canada, Australia, Japan

Cover: Foto ©Thomas Meinert / pixelio.de

More available books at **www.hansebooks.com**

BIBLE

TEMPERANCE

HYMNS.

A choice collection of Songs adapted to the present phase
of the Temperance Work, Sunday-Schools, Prayer
Meetings, and the Home Circle.

BY

J. MERRITTE DRIVER.

———∘∘⟩∘⟨∘∘———

CINCINNATI:

Published by JOHN CHURCH & CO., 66 W. 4th St.

DEDICATION.

TO Doctor Henry Reynolds, Francis Murphy, Thos. L. Noble, M. Lanigan, Thomas Hornbrook, J. C. Bontecou, John A. Drew, Rev. C. E. Page, and the many other noble workers who have willingly and most cheerfully consecrated their lives to the reformation of their fellow beings, this book is most respectfully inscribed.

THE AUTHOR.

PREFACE.

THIS collection has been prepared to supply a need keenly felt by those engaged in the Temperance work, both in the Club and Lodge room, and where "shot and shell were thickest."

Most of the pieces are now for the first time presented to the public, and there is not a single piece included for the mere purpose of "filling up." It has been the aim of the Author to point those struggling in the thralldom of Intemperance to Him "who turneth not away," and who is able and willing to break the shackles of the hydra-headed monster.

With the hope that my labors may, in some degree, aid in the great work of freeing souls from this giant monster, and be instrumental in leading many who are weary and heavy-laden to the dear Redeemer, I commend to the workers, to those struggling for deliverence, and to the Christian people every-where, this collection of " Bible Temperance Hymns for the Camp and Battlefield."

J. MERRITTE DRIVER.

No. 1.   Ho! Sound the Tocsin.

J. M. D.   J. MERRITTE DRIVER.

Maestoso.

1. Ho! sound the toc-sin! shout a-loud, hur-rah! And look up-on the
2. Ho! look, the en-e-my is giv-ing way, Fresh triumphs crown the
3. Ho! sound the toc-sin! far o'er hill and plain! Till from the skies 'tis
4. Then on and on, still fighting, day by day, And while we're fighting

en-e-my's ar-ray; Stay not, nor stop ye! raise again the cry, We fight! we'll
battle of to-day; The shouts are going up from gladdened hearts, While from his
echoed back again; The en-e-my is routed in the fight, God says, "I'm
fail we not to pray; Thus from the demon ever saving men, We'll sing the

CHORUS.

conquer! on to vic-to-ry! Hur-rah! stand firm! Be valiant in the
hold the en-e-my de-parts.
with you, struggling for the right."
chorus—"Praise the Lord, Amen."

fight; God says, "I'm with you, struggling for the right;" Stay not, nor stop ye!

raise again the cry—Fight on! we'll conquer! on to vic-to-ry!

No. 2.　God Help Thee Now to Conquer.

Fanny J. Crosby.

J. Merritte Driver.

1. Nay, touch it not, 'tis poison! Touch not the madd'ning bowl, That
2. Look not with eyes of longing, When gleams the ru-by wine, Or
3. Recoil with deepest loathing From that which blights thy name; That

robs thee of thy reason, And steals away thy soul; Thy best and purest
days of hopeless sorrow And pain will yet be thine; Temptation un-re-
leads to wreck and ruin, To pov-er-ty and shame; Ere yet the lamp of

feelings It turns to bitter hate; Then dash the poison from thee, Or
sist - ed Will lead to crime at last; Oh, let the cross of Je-sus Its
mer - cy For thee shall cease to burn; Oh, fly to him who pities, And

CHORUS.

sad will be thy fate.
shadow o'er thee cast. God help thee, now, to conquer This great and dreadful
longs for thy return.

sin; Oh, seek him at the o - pen door, And he will let thee in.

4

No. 3.   Jesus Loved Me.

JOHN SCOTT, D. D.   J. A. MUNK, M D.

1. Wand'ring in the paths of fol-ly, Without peace, or joy, or rest,
2. With a humble, con-trite spir-it, Mourning on account of sin,
3. In his gen-tle arms he took me, Pressed me to his lov-ing heart—

Je-sus called me, called me to him, That in him I might be blest.
Trust-ing in the Sav-ior's mer-it, Tremblingly I come to him
Doubts and fears at once for-sook me; Je-sus bade them all de-part.

CHORUS.

Je-sus loved me, oh, he loved me! And he's still my lov-ing Friend;

Je-sus loves me, yes, he loves me, And he'll love me to the end.

4 Great the joy his favor gives me,
   Sweet the peace his love inspires,
   Thrilling all my heart with gladness,
   Filling all its vast desires. *Cho.*

5 Trusting in the Savior's merit,
   Clinging to his cross alone,
   Passing through the vale of shadows,
   I shall dwell with him at home. *Cho.*

Webb.

GEO. JAMES WEBB.

1 The morning light is breaking, The darkness disappears; The sons of earth are
2. See heathen nations bending Before the God we love, And thousand hearts as-

wak-ing To pen - i-ten-tial tears. Each breeze that sweeps the o-cean Brings
cending, In grat-i-tude a - bove, While sinners now confessing, The

tid-ings from a-far, Of nations in commotion, Prepared for Zion's war.
gos-pel call o-bey, And seek the Savior's blessing, A nation in a day.

No. 5.   The Temperance Band.

TUNE.—*Webb.*

1 Unfurl the Temp'rance Banner,
  And fling it to the breeze,
And let the glad hosanna
  Sweep over land and seas;
To God be all the glory
  For what we now behold—
Oh, let the cheering story
  In every ear be told.

2 The drunkard shall not perish
  In Alcohol's dire chain,
But wife and children cherish
  Within his home again ;
And sobered men, repenting,
  Will bow at Jesus' feet,
Their thankful hearts relenting
  Before the mercy seat.

3 A new-waked zeal is burning
  In this and every land,
And thousands now are turning
  To join our temp'rance band ;
The light of truth is shining
  In many a darkened soul;
Ere long its rays combining
  Will blaze from pole to pole.

4 Soon will a brighter morrow
  Succeed this pleasant day,
When drink and sin and sorrow
  Shall fly far, far away ;
Then let us swell the chorus,
  And sweeter anthems raise,
While angels bending o'er us,
  Shall join in holy praise.

6

No. 6. Cold Water is our Motto.
TUNE.— *Webb.*

1 Come, swell the ranks of temp'rance,
Let him that heareth come;
Come, brave young men and maidens,
March to the temp'rance drum;
We've listed in the army,
The temp'rance flag we fly,
Cold water is our motto,
And shall be till we die.

2 Come, fathers, sons, and brothers,
Oh, harken to the call!
The bugle blasts of temp'rance
Sound loud and clear to all;
We'll march in solid phalanx,
And raise our banners high;
Cold water is our motto,
And shall be till we die.

No. 7. Stand up for Temperance.
TUNE.— *Webb.*

1 Stand up, stand up for temp'rance,
Ye soldiers of the cross;
Be working! save the fallen
By pointing to the cross;
The sons of earth are sinking
Beneath rum's fearful sway;
Go, thou, and be a doing
Ere fades away the day.

2 Oh, let us work for temp'rance,
And for the cause of right,
That sorrow may be banished
With all its woe and blight;
Put on the gospel armor
And to the battle go,
Resolved to fight till conquered
Shall be this fearful foe.

3 Stand up, stand up for temp'rance,
Stand up and show your might;
Stay not from this great conflict,
Rush now into the fight;
The enemy is wav'ring,
Now harder press the fight;
Wait not a moment longer,
Go, save a soul to-night.

4 Oh, drinker, do not linger
Outside the open door;
You are not free from danger
Till pledged to drink no more;
Before this meeting closes,
Resolve to come and sign;
Perhaps you are the "hundredth,"
Far from the "ninety and nine."

5 And when this step you've taken,
Resolved to be a man,

You'll go forth, free forever,
A better, happier man,
And, up among the angels,
Will sing around the throne,
"Rejoice," the wand'rer's rescued,
"The Lord brings back his own."
J. MERRITTE DRIVER.

No. 8. Temperance Star.
TUNE.— *Webb.*

1 All hail the temperance morning
That dawned with feeble light,
Now bursts with brilliant lustre
On our astonished sight.
Come view the bow of promise,
And see before it fly
The dark clouds of intemperance
That covered all the sky.

2 But now behold! the temperance star
Arose with genial ray,
And, melted by its heavenly warmth,
The thick mist fell away.
Talk ye of slaves who sign the pledge?
We, we alone are free!
Our limbs, our reason ne'er shall bow,
Oh, Alcohol, to thee.
MRS. A. T. H. TAYLOR.

No. 9. The Red Ribbon Army.
TUNE.— *We're a Band of Freemen.*

1 We come, dear friends, to proffer,
Not gold to fill each coffer,
But kindly here to offer
You the Cold Water Pledge.
CHORUS.
We're the Red Ribbon Army,
We're the Red Ribbon Army,
We're the Red Ribbon Army,
And we'll sound it thro' the land.

2 May dram-shops be forsaken,
May all the land awaken,
Stand firmly and unshaken
To our Cold Water Pledge.
Chorus.

3 Oh! come, ye manhood killers,
Ye venders and distillers;
Come, jug and bottle fillers,
Take our Cold Water Pledge.
Chorus.

4 And you, too, bonnie lasses,
Who tip the sparkling glasses,
Right here, before it passes,
Sign our Cold Water Pledge.
Chorus.

5 And boys, with life before you,
May high resolves come o'er you,
Oh! take it, we implore you,
Take our Cold Water Pledge.
Chorus.
KATE HARRINGTON.

No. 10.   The Badge of Blue.

Speak unto the children of Israel, and bid them . . . that they put upon the fringe of
the borders a ribband of blue.—NUMBERS 15 : 38.

J. M. D.   J. MERRITTE DRIVER.

1. The gos-pel blue, The badge that you And ev - 'ry one should wear,
2. You think that some Now in the room Would deem the act ab - surd—
3. With it so pure You'd be se-cure From things that now would tempt;
4. Then come to-night, Do what is right, And don the badge of blue;

Is free for all, Both great and small, Who from strong drink for - bear.
'Tis not the case; They'll take their place, And wear it at a word.
From curse of wine, Tho' bright it shine, Henceforth you'd be ex-empt.
'Twould do you good If now you would Thus show that you are true.

CHORUS. A little faster.

wear . . .

Then come and wear The badge of blue, . . . For-
Then come and wear,   The badge of blue.

more, . . .   true, ...

ev-er-more, For-ev - ermore, Each one so true, Each one so true. Un-

furl your flag, . . .   And show you're on

Unfurl your flag With manly pride, . . .   And
With manly pride,

The Badge of Blue. Concluded.

the Templar's side.

show you're on the Templar's side.

5 Come one and all,
Both great and small,
The high, the rich, the poor,
And from henceforth
Go prove its worth,
And work for thousands more.

No. 11. This Love so Free.

"To the Young Ladies' Christian Working Band," Monticello, Iowa.

M. M. J.   Behold, what manner of love.—1 JOHN 3: 1.   MARK M. JONES, by per.

1. How tenderly Je-sus loves us, With love so pure and free,
2. His love so free-ly giv-en, Was purchas'd by his blood,
3. Be-neath that pur-ple fount-ain, That flows from Jesus' side,
4. And now the Sav-ior begs us This precious love re-ceive,

Down from his throne a-bove us, It comes to you and me.
That from his dear side riv-en Pours forth a sav-ing flood.
Down o-ver Cal-v'ry's mountain We safe-ly may a-bide.
And all that it will cost us, Is sim-ply to be-lieve.

CHORUS.

Oh, who can con-ceive it, Oh, who can be-lieve it,

Oh, who will re-ceive it, This love so free?

9

No. 12. Come, Friends and Brethren.

TUNE.—*Auld Lang Syne.*

1. Come, friends and brethren, all unite, In songs of hearty cheer; Our cause speed onward
2. The cup of death no more we take; That cup no more we give; It makes the head, the

CHORUS.

in its might, Away with doubt and fear. We give the pledge, we join the hand, Re-
bosom ache—Ah! who can drink and live.

solved on victory; We are a bold, determined band, And strike for liberty.

No. 13. Auld Acquaintance.

TUNE.—*Auld Lang Syne.*

1 Should auld acquaintance be forgot,
   Who've fallen by the way?
   Should we, who know a happier lot
   Leave them in grief to stay?
   Though rough the fortune they have
      met,
   From tasting ruin's cup,
   They are our erring brothers yet,
   And we will lift them up.

2 Then still press on; sublime the aim
   In which we all combine,—
   To rescue man from sin and shame,
   That he in heaven may shine.
   That welcome, welcome, ever blessed,
   May fall upon the ear,
   Of those whose hearts have been op-
      pressed
   With sin and sorrow here.

No. 14. Cold Water Army.

TUNE.—*Auld Lang Syne.*

1 With banner and with badge we come,
   An army true and strong;
   To fight against the hosts of rum,
   And this shall be our song.

   CHORUS.

   We love the clear cold water springs,
      Supplied by gentle showers;
   We feel the strength cold water brings,
      The victory is ours.

2 "Cold Water Army" is our name,
   Oh, may we faithful be,
   And so in truth and justice claim
   The blessings of the free. *Cho.*

3 Tho' others love their Rum and Wine,
   And drink till they are mad;
   To water we will still incline,
   To make us strong and glad. *Cho.*

No. 15. We'll give up the Social Drink, Boys.

J. M. D.

J. MERRITTE DRIVER.

1. I have drank the so-cial glass, boys, I have drank the so-cial cup;
2. Oft in rev-el-ry and song, boys, When the glow of morn was nigh,
3. Oh, it was that dread de-sire, boys, Thirsting for the sparkling wine,
4. Seeing plain the fi-nal end, boys, And how near to ru-in's edge,

And to ru-in I'd have gone, boys, If I had not giv'n it up.
I have tipp'd the cup a-gain, boys, And have drain'd it with a sigh.
That so rul'd my inmost soul, boys, Robb'd me of my ver-y mind.
I'd al-read-y found my way, boys, I have come and sign'd the pledge.

CHORUS.

We'll be happier, we'll be merrier, We'll give up the so-cial drink;

You'll be happier, you'll be merrier, If you'll stop, my boys, and think.

11

No. 16. How Can You Drink Again?

J. McP.

JOHN McPHERSON, by per.

1. How can you drink a-gain, my friend, And know of all the pain
2. Oh, think of wife and children dear, Who plead with you to-night,
3. Yes, now re-solve to quit for all This curse that ru-ins you,

And sin in which the course must end, How can you drink again?
Come, sign the pledge, drink wa-ter clear, And make your household bright;
And break the bands that now enthrall, And don for aye the blue;

It makes a man un-fit to live, And more un-fit to die,
Your children then up-on your knee, Will love you as of yore,
You'll live a hap-py, prosp'rous life, Perhaps unknown to fame,

How Can You Drink Again? Concluded.

Then why will you the cup re-ceive, Pray tell me, drinker, why?
And your dear wife will hap - py be To meet you at the door.
But when you're gone from sin and strife, Your child will bless your name.

CHORUS.

How can you drink a-gain? How can you drink a - gain?

How can you drink a - gain? . . How can you drink a - gain?

How can you drink a - gain? . . a - gain?

Come, help us win poor souls from sin, And nev-er drink a - gain.

Come, help us win poor souls from sin, And nev-er drink a - gain.

13

No. 17. Something To Do.

"Go work to-day in my vineyard."—MATT. 21: 28.

J. M. D.   J. MERRITTE DRIVER.

1. Something to do—has been ring-ing to-day, Fill-ing my heart with a
2. Something to do—oh, most glo-rious tho't, Now I praise God for this
3. Something to do—may this tho't ev-er be Ring-ing a-far on a
4. Something to do—send us forth in thy cause, Bless us as dai-ly we

won-der-ful joy; Blessing my soul as hour-ly I pray, Make me a
heav-enly theme; Making my work the wan-der-er sought, Mak-ing my
life-giving wave; Make each one feel that now we must be Working each
la-bor for thee; Grant, oh, at last, thy rich-est applause, When at thy

CHORUS.

ser-vant in thy employ.
song His pow'r to redeem.   We praise thee, we praise thee for something to
hour that souls we may save.
throne dear Jesus we see.

do, Dear Je-sus, we glad-ly are working for you; Oh, bless us, and

guide us with infini'e love, And grant oh, at last, a sure entrance a-bove.

No. 18.   Do I Refuse?

VIRGINIA J. KENT.   LUCY J. RIDER.

Resolute.

1. Do I re-fuse? 'Tis but a glass of sparkling wine, Yet un-told
2. Do I re-fuse? By tho't of all these bitter years, By woman's
3. Do I re-fuse? Yes, by these memories of old, By sor-rows
4. Do I re-fuse? Yes, in the strength of God, I do, I'll to my

With expression.

woes for me and mine, Within its depths of ruby shine—I do re-fuse!
hopes, by children's tears, My mother's agonizing prayers—I do re-fuse!
deep and all untold, By all my wasted time and gold—I do re-fuse!
solemn vow be true, This cup of trembling and of woe—I do re-fuse!

CHORUS.

hang on the an-swer of this

My joy in life, my hope in death, May hang up-on this

fleeting breath, God help me now my words to choose, I do! I do re-fuse!

No. 19. "Don't Stay Late To-night."

ANON.

J. A. MUNK, M D.

With feeling.

1. The hearth of home is beam - ing With rays of ros - y
2. The world in which thou mov - est Is bus - y, brave, and
3. The world so cold, in - hu - man, Will spurn thee if thou

light, . . And love - ly eyes are gleam - ing, As
wide; . . The world of her thou lov - est, Is
fall; . . . The love of one poor wo - man, Out-

fall the shades of night; And while thy steps are
on - ly at thy side; She waits for the warm
lasts and shames them all. Thy children will cling a-

leav - ing The cir - cle pure and bright, . . A
greet - ing, Thy smile is her de - light, . . Her
round thee, Let fate be dark or bright, . . At

plaintive voice, en-treat - ing, Says, "Don't stay late to - night."
plaintive voice, en-treat - ing, Says, "Don't stay late to - night."
home no shaft will wound thee, Then "Don't stay late to - night."

CHORUS.

"Don't stay late to - night," . . Oh, "Don't stay late to - night;"

to - night,

Rit.

A plaintive voice en-treat-ing-ly, Says, "Don't stay late to - night."

2

17

No. 20. Missionary Hymn.
TUNE.—*Don't Stay Late To-night, p. 16.*

1 Oh! patiently we've waited
   To see the happy day,
   When man shall tempt his brother
   No more to go astray;
   And all shall strive together
   To lift the fallen up,
   And teach the weak and wretched
   To leave the cruel cup.

2 With words and deeds of kindness,
   With words of love and cheer,
   Oh! treat thy fellow being,
   Through all his trials here.
   There's poverty and sorrow
   Wherever we may go;
   Then let us, like the angels,
   Be kind to all below.

3 Be true to all the living,
   For but a transient hour,
   And love and comfort giving,
   Will be beyond our power.
   Give misery our pity,
   And treat our fellow man
   As though he were our brother,
   And help him while we can.

No. 21. Temperance Hymn.
TUNE.—*Don't Stay Late To-night.*

1 From brightest crystal fountain,
   That flows in beauty free
   By shady hill and mountain,
   Fill high the cup for me!
   Sing of the sparkling waters
   Sing of the cooling spring—
   Let freedom's sons and daughters
   Their joyous tribute bring.

2 This was the pledge in Eden,
   Ere sorrow's notes were heard;
   Ere our first mother heeding
   The subtle serpent's word—
   Forgetting her Creator,
   Plunged all her race in woe,
   And caused o'er beauteous Nature
   The seeds of death to grow.

3 From many a happy dwelling
   Late misery's dark abode,
   The joyous peal is swelling—
   The hymn of praise to God,
   Glad songs are now ascending
   From many a thankful heart;
   Hope, Joy, and Peace are blending
   And each their aid impart.

4 We'll join the tuneful chorus
   And raise our song on high!

The cheering view before us
Delights the raptured eye;
The glorious cause is gaining
   New strength from day to day,
The drunkard host is waning
   Before cold water's sway.

No. 22. Can I E'er Drink Again.
TUNE.—*When the Swallows Homeward Fly.*

1 When my little weeping child
   Is bowed down with grief so wild,
   When my wife in deep despair,
   Pleads for me with words of prayer,
   When I see each haggard face,
   Know that drink doth joy erase,
   When I all these wrongs do see,
   Can I, ah, can I e'er drink again?
   Can I, ah, can I e'er drink again?

2 When I think of boyhood days,
   With their round of merry plays,
   When from father, mother dear,
   Came their warning with a tear,
   When of sisters, too, I think,
   And my life with theirs do link,
   When I all their tears do see,
   Can I, ah, can I e'er drink again?
   Can I, ah, can I e'er drink again?

3 No! I'll never drink again,
   From this hour I'll be a man,
   And I'll wipe away those tears,
   Giving joy through coming years,
   By-and-by there'll dawn a day,
   When silently we'll pass away,
   When I all these things do know,
   I pray I may never drink again,
   I pray I may never drink again!
                              J. MERRITTE DRIVER.

No. 23. Parting Blessing.
TUNE.—*Greenville.*

1 Heavenly father, give thy blessing,
   While we now this meeting end,
   On our minds each truth impressing
   That may to thy glory tend.

2 Save from all intoxication,
   From its fountains may we flee,
   When assailed by strong temptation
   Put our trust alone in thee.

No. 24. Doxology.

Be thou, O God, exalted high;
And as thy glory fills the sky,
So let it be on earth displayed,
Till thou art here as there obeyed.

No. 25. America.

1. My coun-try, 'tis of thee, Sweet land of lib - er - ty,
2. My na - tive coun - try, thee, Land of the no - ble free,
3. Let mu - sic swell the breeze, And ring from all the trees
4. Our fa - ther's God! to thee, Au - thor of lib - er - ty,

Of thee I sing; Land where my fa - thers died, Land of the
Thy name I love; I love thy rocks and rills, Thy woods and
Sweet free-dom's song; Let mor - tal tongues a-wake, Let all that
To thee we sing; Long may our land be bright With freedom's

pil - grim's pride, From ev-'ry mount-ain side, Let free-dom ring.
tem - pled hills, My heart with rap-ture thrills Like that a - bove.
breathe partake, Let rocks their silence break, The sound pro-long.
ho - ly light, Pro-tect us by thy might, Great God, our King!

No. 26. Invocation.

TUNE.—*America.*

1 We come, great God, to thee,
In deep humility,
  Thy help implore;
And as we humbly wait,
Our hearts we consecrate
To thee, who art so great,
  For evermore.

2 Here we our pledges take,
Intemperance to forsake,
  While life doth last;
Save from this deadly foe,
That crushes man so low,
From all the shame and woe
  Of our sad past.

No. 27. The Pledge for All.

TUNE.—*America.*

1 My country, 'tis for thee,
Whose boast is liberty,
  For thee I pray;
Land, for whose fair domain,
The tyrant's ruthless chain
Reached out and sought in vain
  To bind for aye.

2 In wan despair they stand;
The Rachels of our land,
  And wildly call:
"Oh, friends! arouse! awake!
The ranks of Satan break,
And this your war-cry make,
  'The pledge for all!'"

KATE HARRINGTON.

No. 28. Father's a Drunkard.

ANON. J. MERRITTE DRIVER,

With feeling.

1. Out in the gloomy night sad-ly I roam, I have no mother
2. We were so hap-py till fa-ther drank rum, Then all our sor-rows
3. Oh, if the temp'rance men would on-ly find Poor wretched father,

dear, no pleasant home; No one cares for me, no one would cry,
and trouble be-gun; Mother grew pale and wept ev-'ry day—
and talk ver-y kind; If they would stop him from drinking, why then,

Ev-en if poor lit-tle Bes-sie would die. Wea-ry and
Ba-by and I were too hun-gry to play. Slow-ly they
I should be so ver-y hap-py a-gain! Is it too

20 Copyright, 1878, by John Church & Co.

Father's a Drunkard. Concluded.

tired, I've been wand'ring all day, Ask - ing for work, but I'm
fad - ed, till one sum-mer night Found their dead fac - es all
late, temp'rance men ? please try, Or poor little Bes - sie must

too small they say; On the damp ground I must lay my
si - lent and white; Then with big tears slow-ly drop - ping, I
soon starve and die; All the day long I've been beg - ging for

Rit.

head, Fa - ther's a drunkard, and moth-er is dead.
said, Fa - ther's a drunkard, and moth-er is dead.
bread— Fa - ther's a drunkard, and moth-er is dead.

Rit. e Dim.

25

No. 29. Temperance Rallying Song.

"Fight the good fight of faith."

1. Fill the ranks with soldiers and be ready for the fight, Let the world be-
2. Fill the ranks with soldiers, we will never be afraid, First in ev - 'ry

hold us with our colors waving bright; We're the temp'rance army, and we
conflict where the tempter would invade; Bringing back the sunlight o'er the

bat-tle for the right, As we go marching on. Ral-ly, rally round the
ru - in he has made, Oh, we'll go marching on.

Ral-ly, ral - ly

stand - ard! Ral - ly, ral - ly round the stand - ard!

round the stand-ard! Ral - ly, ral - ly round the stand-ard!

Ral-ly, ral-ly round the stand - ard, As we go marching on!

Ral-ly, ral - ly round the standard, As we go marching on!

No.30. Rally, let us Rally.
TUNE.—Glory, Hallelujah.

1 Rally, let us rally and for temperance boldly stand,
Shout the cry to battle, send the call to every land;
Rally, let us rally with the sword of God in hand,
And all be marching on;
Glory, Hallelujah,
Praise God, we're marching on.

2 See the prince of darkness in his haughty pride arrayed,
Mark the desolation by his deadly poison made,
He must fall before us, and the ruin must be stayed,
The brave are marching on,
Glory Hallelujah, etc,

3 Oh, the nightly revels and the money squandered there,
Plunging homes in darkness and the anguish of despair;
Father, save the fallen—is our heartfelt, earnest prayer,
To conquest marching on.
Glory Hallelujah, etc.

4 By the tears of suffering in the wretched mother's eyes,
By her helpless children and their plaintive, starving cries,
Oh, by every feeling that is sacred, let us rise
For temperance marching on.
Glory Hallelujah, etc.

5 Though the fierce avenger with his army now assail,
Dauntless we will face them, for in God we shall prevail,
Trusting Him to lead us, we shall never, never fail,
Then boldly we'll march on.
Glory Hallelujah, etc.
FANNY J. CROSBY.

No.31. Crusader's Battle Hymn.
TUNE.—Glory Hallelujah.

1 The light of truth is breaking,
On the mountain tops it gleams,
Let it flash along the valleys,
Let it glitter on our streams,
Till all our land awakens,
In its flush of golden beams;
Our God is marching on.
CHORUS,—Glory, glory, hallelujah, etc.

2 From morning's early watches,
Till the setting of the sun,
We will never flag nor falter
In the work we have begun,
Till the forts have all surrendered,
And the victory is won,—
The time is marching on.—CHO.

3 We wield no carnal weapons,
And we hurl no fiery dart,
But with words of love and reason,
We are sure to win the heart,
And persuade the poor transgressor
To prefer the better part,—
Our God is marching on.—CHO.

No.32. Say, Brothers.
TUNE.—Glory, Hallelujah.

1 Say, brothers, will you join us?
Say, brothers, will you join us?
Say, brothers, will you join us?
As we go marching on?

CHORUS:—Glory, glory, hallelujah,
Glory, glory, hallelujah,
Glory, glory, hallelujah,
As we go marching on.

2 By the help of God we'll join you,
By the help of God we'll join you,
By the help of God we'll join you,
By the help of God we'll join you,
And with you march along.

3 We will boldly strike for freedom,
We will boldly strike for freedom,
We will boldly strike for freedom,
And shake off the chains of rum.

4 We have join'd the conqu'ring legion,
We have join'd the conqu'ring legion,
We have join'd the conqu'ring legion,
And are marching up to heaven.
KATE HARRINGTON.

23

The Call of the Loved Ones. Concluded.

CHORUS. Legato.

Sopr.
God is now waiting . . your vow to re-ceive, . . He will now save, . .

Tenor & Alto.
God is now waiting your vow to receive, He will now

Bass.

. . . . if you will believe ; Turn to him quick - ly, his promises claim,

save, if you will believe ; Turn to him quickly, his promises claim,

Rit. **Rit.**
Tho' you have sinned, . . he loveth the same, Loveth the same.

Rit. e Dim.
Tho' you have sinned, he loveth the same, loveth the same.

5 Come, oh, come quickly, my brother!
    The day-beams are sinking afar,
There never is given another,
    And soon sets the bright evening star!
Quickly determine to come,
    And walk in the path of the right,
Turn from a terrible doom,
    And loved ones will bless you—will bless you to-night. *Cho.*

No. 34. The Temperance Banner.

Rev. E. T. B.
Rev. E. T. Bowers.

1. See the Temp'rance Banner wav-ing, And the ar-my marching
2. We will ral-ly round the standard, Ev-er dare to do the
3. As the contest round us rag-es, Let us lift the ban-ner

on, (marching on;) In the breeze its folds are streaming, It shall
right, (do the right;) Till the Rum-king's hosts are conquered, And his
high, (lift it high;) For the foe is now re-treat-ing, And the

CHORUS.

wave till vic-t'ry's won.
le-gions put to flight.   Let it wave, ev - er
time of tri-umph's nigh.

Let it wave,

wave, O'er the land and o'er the sea; Let it

ev - er wave, o'er the sea,

wave, ev - er wave, Till we gain the vic-to-ry.

Let it wave, ev - er wave,

The Tainted Cup.

Rev. D. B Dorsey.   Dr. J. A. Munk.

1. Pure thro' the veins the life tide flows, From the fountain of the heart;
2. Pure in the mind the tho'ts a - rise From founts that are deep within,
3. Pure in the soul good purposes flow From fountains that are divine,
4. Sweet-ly the tide of life flows on, With flowers on ei-ther brink,

It needs no aid from the vintner's skill, No help from the brewer's art.
But the demon of drink corrupts those founts, And the tho'ts are stained with sin.
But the purest and best are fatally soiled, By the curse that lurks in the wine.
But the tide grows murky, the flowers die, 'Neath the fatal curse of drink.

CHORUS.

Then dash a - way the brimming cup, Taste not its curse ma-lign;

The healthful cur - rent of the blood Is taint - ed by the wine.

No. 36. Touch not the Cup.

TUNE.—*Long, Long Ago.*

1 Touch not the cup, it is death to thy
soul,
Touch not the cup, touch not the cup;
Many I know who have quaffed from
the bowl,
Touch not the cup, touch it not;
Little they thought that the demon
was there,
Blindly they drank and were caught
in the snare,
Then of that death-dealing bowl, oh !
beware.
Touch not the cup, touch it not.

2 Touch not the cup, young man in
thy pride,
Touch not the cup, touch not the cup;
Hark to the warning of thousands
who've died,
Touch not the cup, touch it not;
Go to their lonely and desolate tomb;
Think of their death, of their sorrow
and gloom,
Think that perhaps you may share
in their doom,
Touch not the cup, touch it not.

3 Touch not the cup, oh ! drink not a drop,
Touch not the cup, touch not the cup;
All that thou lovest entreat thee to stop,
Touch not the cup, touch it not;
Stop, for the home that to thee is so near,
Stop, for the home that to thee is so dear,
Stop, for thy country, the God that
you fear,
Touch not the cup, touch it not;

No. 37. Marching Along.

1 The army of temperance is gathering
its men,
From hill-top and mountain, in val-
ley and glen ;
Cold water's our bev'rage we are
lusty and strong,
Then come join our army and be
marching along.
CHORUS.—Marching along—we are
marching along,
Come join our army and be march-
ing along ;
Cold water will make us both val-
iant and strong,
Then come join our army and be
marching along.

2 From mountain to lakes, from the
gulf to the strand,
Our army is marching in strength
through the land,

In love, faith, and purity, we still
will grow strong,
Then come join our army and be
marching along.—CHO.

No. 38. The Battle Cry of Temperance.

TUNE.—*The Battle Cry of Freedom.*

1 We will rally in our might
To the great and glorious fight,
Shouting the battle cry of temperance.
We will deal a final blow
To the mean, insidious foe,
Shouting the battle cry of temperance.
CHORUS.—Cold water forever ! away
with the wine,
For us its false glitter no longer
shall shine,
We will rally in our might
To the great and glorious fight,
Shouting the battle cry of temperance.

2 Long has alcohol held sway,
Now we'll drive the fiend away,
Shouting the battle cry of temperance.
We will break the poisonous bowl
Which will ruin mind and soul,
Shouting the battle cry of temper-
ance !—CHO.

3 Now's the day and now's the hour,
Let us break wine's wicked power,
Shouting the battle cry of temperance.
Gird the armor on anew,
Be in earnest and be true,
Shouting the battle cry of temper-
ance !—CHO.

No. 39. Friends of Temperance.

1 Friends of temperance, quick to arms,
We must struggle for the right ;
And our noble cause with vigor
we'll defend,
See the foe is gaining ground,
We must meet him in the fight,
And be faithful and courageous to
the end.
CHORUS.—Marching onward, ever
onward,
Sounding still the battle cry ;
Soon the tyrant shall be slave,
To our army bold and brave !
We shall gain a glorious victory by
and by.

2 Like the fatal wind that sweeps,
O'er the desert's burning plain,
Is the deep and deadly poison of his breath,
While the aged and the young,
He is binding with a chain,
That will lead them on by thou-
sands down to death.

No. 40. Oh, How Sweet 'tis to Toil!

MRS. ANNIE HOWE THOMSON. J. A. MUNK, M. D.

1. Oh, how sweet 'tis to toil For the Mas-ter be-low, Thro' the sunshine and shade of the years! Tho' the vines that we plant, And the seed that we sow, Are but wa-tered full oft with our tears. Tho' our spirits grow faint 'Neath the burden we bear, And with longings we turn to our rest; Yet what comforts descend With the whispers of pray'r,

2. Oh, how sweet 'tis to toil For the Mas-ter be-low, E'en thro' the tri-als, thro' sorrows and pain! Tho' we nev-er may reap Of the har-vest we sow, And no glo-ry on earth we may gain. If a-bid-ing each day 'Neath the shade of his wing, If we're sheltered at last on yon shore; Oh, were that not enough For the fruits that we bring,

Oh, How Sweet 'tis to Toil. Concluded.

CHORUS.

Oh, what peace to each storm-driven breast! Oh, how sweet 'tis to
And to wak-en our praise ev-er-more! Oh, how sweet

toil ('tis to toil) For the Mas-ter be-low, Tho' the vines that we plant

And the seeds that we sow, Are but watered full oft with our tears.

No. 41. Save the Children.

"For of such is the kingdom of heaven."

AIR.—*Scatter Seeds of Kindness.*

1 Let us gather in the children
  With a loving, gentle band;
  Let us save them from intemperance,
  In a holy, happy band;
  Let us guard them in their childhood
  From the danger of the way;
  From the demon let us shield them,
  While the danger's far away.
    CHORUS.
  Then let us save the children,
  Then let us save the children,
  Then let us save the children,
  For his kingdom by and by.

2 Well we know the demon labors,
  Working hourly to o'erthrow;
  Let us strike him from his stronghold,
  Urged on by the drunkard's woe;
  Let us save the lambs around us
  Ere the demon shall enthrall;
  Listen to them loudly calling,
  Come and save us e'er we fall.
    CHORUS.

3 Strange that we should slight the
    children,
  While they gather round our board,
  Strange we tell them not of danger,
  From the demon and his horde,
  Strange, that knowing childhood
    passeth,
  Soon we feel the evening dew
  That we fail to tell of danger,
  And to urge them to be true.
    CHORUS.

4 Ah! the drunkard reeling, falling,
  How he points our mem'ries back
  To the days of happy childhood,
  Ere he left the narrow track,
  When the words of gentle warning,
  Kindly given him day by day,
  Might have saved him from thus
    falling
  From a *drunkard's doom* that day.
    CHORUS

  J. MERRITTE DRIVER.

33

No. 42. Almost Persuaded.

NEW WORDS.

1 Almost persuaded, now to be free,
Almost persuaded, God helping me,
Now from the social glass,
Now from the wretched past,
Into the light at last,
God helping me.

2 Almost persuaded, ah! galling chain,
Almost persuaded, strive I in vain,
To break its iron band,
To leave the fearful strand,
To gain sweet freedom's land,
Man helping me.

3 Almost persuaded, ah! bitter wail,
Almost persuaded, can it avail?
Hear, hear a sister's cry,
Ah! see the wife's sad eye,
Listen to a mother's sigh,
Will they avail?

4 Almost persuaded, ah! fearful woe,
Almost persuaded, can I e'er know,
Know all the widow's life,
All in its daily strife,
With dire forebodings rife,
Would I abstain.

5 Fully persuaded, can I be free,
Fully persuaded, God helping me,
Free from the galling chain,
Free from the bitter shame,
Free ever to remain,
God helping me.

GEO. DEW.

No. 43. The Right Shall Prevail.

TUNE.—*Sweet By and By.*

1 When the right over wrong shall prevail,
When the woes of wine drinking
shall cease,
Then all nations and people shall
hail
With a shout the grand triumph
of peace.

CHORUS.

It will come by and by,
When the race out of childhood is
grown;
It will come by and by,
Then the age of true manhood
shall dawn.

2 Right ordains that the old wrongs
cease,
And make way for the growth of
reform;
Truth and wisdom proclaim, from
on high,
That the triumph of virtue must
come.

CHORUS.

3 It will come by and by,
When the sway of foul passion is
o'er;
It will come by and by,
Then fair reason shall rule evermore.

No. 44. A Glorious Day.

TUNE.—*Sweet By and By.*

1 There is dawning a glorious day,
Its light may it quickly appear,
With drunkenness banished away,
What hopes will our hearts sweetly
cheer.

CHORUS.

Let us work for that day,
For that glorious temperance day,
Let us work for that day,
For that glorious temperance day.

2 The lab'rers are now in the field,
And the harvest is ready to reap,
Come and share in this glorious
yield,
Your reward doth your master now
keep.—CHO.

3 The demons of darkness are near,
And our loved ones are struggling
to-day,
Oh! impelled by the greatest of fear,
Let us drive now this tyrant away.
CHO.

4 If we fail—in the great coming day,
When to us will be given our lot,
The voice of the Father will say,
Go! Depart from me, I know you not.
CHO.

5 Then let us be working till death,
Till below shall be ended our
strife,
When above will be given a wreath,
With a crown of rejoicing and
life.—CHO.

J. MERRITTE DRIVER.

No. 45. Rescue the Drunkard.

J. McP.   JOHN MCPHERSON.

1. Rescue the man who to dram-shops will go, Try to convince him to-night;
2. Ask him to think of his household, once bright, Now filled with sadness and gloom;
3. Beg of him, plead with him, ask him to think, Sad will his ending be;

Show him that rum is his deadliest foe, Point him the way that is right.
Mother and children are pleading to-night, That he may sober come home.
Come, be a man now, and never more drink, From the glass e'er more be free.

CHORUS.

Rescue the drunkard, work night and day, Never the battle give o'er;

Oh, hear his children pleading-ly say, "Oh, father, drink no more!"

3   33

No. 46. Glorious News.

Original.

L. O. EMERSON, by per.

1. Oh, have you heard the glorious news That's round the town to-day?
2. Many's the sorrowing time we've had, But such we'll have no more, For
3. Now, thanks we raise to God on high, For this great blessing giv'n; And

Father has signed the pledge, and we Are happy, light and gay.   No
father has driven the demon out, And lock'd and barr'd the door.   No
earth to us hence-forth shall be The en-trance door to heav'n.   Sing

more we dread   his com-ing step, But spring   to greet him home; Moth-
more we'll want for food and clothes, No more we'll mourn and sigh; Our
loud and full,   sing clear and free, Let hill   to val-ley   call,   And

Glorious News. Concluded.

ther has wiped her tears a - way, And joy to us has come.
home shall be a home of peace, With ev-'ry com-fort nigh.
bear up - on the wings of wind, The glorious news to all.

CHORUS.

Oh, glo-rious news, glo-rious news, glo-rious news to - day!

Fa-ther has signed the pledge, and we Are hap-py, light and gay,

Happy, happy, happy, light and gay, Happy, happy, happy, light and gay;

Fa-ther has signed the pledge, And we are hap-py, light and gay.

No. 47. The Temperance Wave.

J. McP.   JOHN McPHERSON.

1. The temp'rance wave, oh, may it roll O'er all our land so bright;
2. It's com-ing on, so bold and free, Submerg-ing in its course
3. It ga-thers work-ers ev-'ry-where, And rules with might-y power;

And may it flow from pole to pole, And rescue homes from blight.
The drunkard in his rev-el ry, And mak-ing hearts re-joice.
Its ben-e-fits we all may share Each pass-ing day and hour.

CHORUS.

The temp'rance wave, oh, may it roll,   Its good we all can see;
The temp'rance wave, oh, may it roll

And let us work with heart and soul Till from rum's curse we're free.
And let us work with heart and soul

Who hath Sorrow?

"They that tarry long at the wine."

PLEYEL.

1. Who hath sorrow? who hath woe? Who hath babbling? who hath strife?
2. They that tar -ry at the wine, They that love the feast and song;
3. Drinker, turn and leave the bowl, Drunkards can not en - ter heav'n;

Who to swift de-struc - tion go, Turn-ing from the path of life?
They that fie - ry drinks com-bine—Ear - ly haste, and tar - ry long.
Christ hath died to save thy soul, Flee to him and be for - giv'n.

No. 49. The Prodigal Invited.
TUNE.—*Pleyel's Hymn.*

1 Brother, hast thou wandered far
From thy Father's happy home,
With thyself and God at war?
Turn thee, brother; homeward come.

2 Hast thou wasted all the powers
God for noble uses gave?
Squandered life's most golden hours?
Turn thee, brother; God can save.

3 He can heal the deepest wound,
He thy gentlest prayer can hear;

Seek him, for he may be found;
Call upon him; he is near.

No. 50. Hark! the Voice.
TUNE.—*Pleyel's Hymn.*

1 Hark! the voice of choral song
Floats upon the breeze along,
Chanting clear, in solemn lays,
"Man redeemed, to God the praise."

2 Courage! let no heart despair,
Mighty is the truth we bear;
Forward, then, baptized in love,
Led by wisdom from above.

No. 51. Stain not the Lips with Ruby Wine.

J. M. D.   J. MERRITTE DRIVER.

1. The wave is roll-ing far and wide, Abstainers now are at the front;
2. Oh, to this work let all a-wake, And strive, with earnest, pray'rful hearts,
3. Stain not the lips with ruby wine; O drink-er of the cup, beware!
4. You now have suffer'd long enough From dreadful whisky's crime and sin;

Who here is on the Templar's side? Who'll now his dreadful foe confront?
Each drunkard from his dream to wake, Till in his grief the teardrops start.
Too LATE, too late you'll sadly find You're bound within a fa-tal snare.
Our Sav-ior cries, "It is enough; Cease now, and I will let you in."

The "Murphy movement" it is call'd; Oh, may its mighty wave roll on!
Oh, let us plead with him each hour, Until his word and pledge be giv'n.
But leave the bright de-lu-sive cup, Re-solve no more to drink the wine
Then pass the pledge from hand to hand, Let each one sign it now, to-night,

* "Reynolds," or "Temp'rance" may be substituted.

Stain not the Lips, etc. Concluded.

'Twill save the hundredth one enthrall'd, And bless us rich-'y ev-'ry one.
Un - til he'll say, I'll drink no more—I pledge it in the hope of heav'n.
God now will save if you'll give up, And trust his pow'r and grace divine.
And form a bright and happy band, Who trust in God and do the right.

CHORUS.

And God will give his help-ing hand, And lend his
He'll make a ho - - ly, hap- py band Of what was

And God will give his helping hand, And lend his
He'll make a ho - ly, hap-py band Of what was

And God will give his helping hand,
He'll make a bright and happy band

1st time.	2d time.

all - - supporting grace;
call'd the [Omit. . . . . .]drunkard's race. . . .

all - - supporting grace;
call'd the [Omit. . . . . .] drunkard's race, the drunkard's race.

And lend his all- - supporting grace;
Of what was call'd [Omit. . . . . .] the drunkard's race.

No. 52. Rally Round the Banner.

GEO. W. BUNGAY.   J. MERRITTE DRIVER.

Spirited.

1. Rally round the temp'rance banner, Wake the echoes with your song;
2. Rally round the temp'rance banner, In the war against this foe,
3. Rally round the temp'rance banner, On the hill-tops let it wave;

Shake the hills with your ho-san-na, Swell the chorus loud and long.
Who will lead the glorious vanguard? Who will deal the conq'ring blow?
Young and old with loud ho-san-na, Cheer the hearts ye toil to save.

Onward still the cause is speeding, Soon will dawn a brighter day,
Strike now, in and out of season, Dash a-side the poison bowl;
Wives and children, join your praises, Fill the air with glad re-frain,

Where hu-man-i-ty lies bleeding, Temp'rance soon shall win the sway.
Save im-mor-tal man his rea-son, Strike the fetters from his soul.
As the daf-fo-dils and daisies Breathe their perfume after rain.

40

No. 53. What shall the Harvest be?

P. P. B.

P. P. Bliss.

1. Sowing the seed by the daylight fair, Sowing the seed by the noonday glare,
2. Sowing the seed by the wayside high, Sowing the seed on the rocks to die,
3. Sowing the seed of a lingering pain, Sowing the seed of a maddened brain,

Sowing the seed by the fad-ing light,   Sowing the seed in the solemn night;
Sowing the seed where the thorns will spoil, Sowing the seed in the fertile soil;
Sowing the seed of a tarnished name, Sowing the seed of e - ter-nal shame;

Oh, what shall the harvest be?   Oh, what shall the harvest be?
Oh, what shall the harvest be?   Oh, what shall the harvest be?
Oh, what shall the harvest be?   Oh, what shall the harvest be?

41

Sown . . . in the dark - - ness or sown . . in the

Sown in the darkness or sown in the light, Sown in the darkness or

light, ... Sown . . . . in our weak - - ness or

sown in the light, Sown in our weakness or sown in our might,

sown . . . . in our might, . . . Gath - ered in time or e-

Sown in our weakness or sown in our might, Gathered in time or e-

ter - ni - ty, Sure, ah, sure will the har - vest be.

ter - ni - ty, Sure, ah, sure will the har - vest, harvest be.

4 Sowing the seed with an aching heart,
Sowing the seed while the tear-drops start,
Sowing in hope till the reapers come,
Gladly to gather the harvest home;
Oh, what shall the harvest be?
Oh, what shall the harvest be?
  Sown in the darkness, etc.

No. 54. Stand Firm for Temperance.

R. R. WADE.   H. S. PERKINS. By per.

SOLO, or all in unison.
With vigor.   CHORUS. *f*

1. Stand firm for temp'rance, nobly stand, "Firm as a rock on ocean's strand;"
2. Stand firm for temp'rance, nobly stand, Send forth the tidings thro' the land;

SOLO.   CHORUS.

Beat back the tid-al wave of woe, Whose surging billows o - ver-flow.
Till every tongue with praise shall sing The wondrous triumph of our King.

CHORUS. *ff*

Stand firm for temp'rance, nobly stand, "Firm as a rock on ocean's strand;"

Gird on your armor for the right, And join your comrades in the fight.

3 Stand firm for temp'rance, nobly stand,
   Our cause is just—in God we trust;
   Come sign the pledge, and join our band,
   And drive our foe from out the land. *Cho.*

43

No. 55.   Only a Child.

[To Mr. and Mrs. T. L. Noble, ("Happy Tom Noble,") of Wheeling, West Virginia.]

J. M. D.   J. MERRITTE DRIVER.

Con Molto Espressione.

1. Only a sis-ter pleading to-night, Heart overcome with bitterest woe;
2. Only a wife that's pleading to-night, Only a wife with galling sad tears;
3. Only a child that's pleading to-night, Only a child in tatters and rags;
4. Oh, 'tis your Savior pleading to-night, Knocking and asking that he may come in;

Long-ing to see you turn to the right, Long-ing that you your
On - ly a wife so ten-der and true, Faithful thro' all these
Say - ing, O fa - ther, turn to the right, List to your child while
Sin - ner, one mo - ment look at the sight, Haste then to save your-

danger may know. See her entreat the Fa - ther a - bove, A
weary long years. List to her voice while weeping she says, O
sad-ly she begs. Fa - ther, O fa - ther, sad 'tis to think, How
self from your sin. Lo! hear him plead on Cal - va - ry's brow, He'll

Only a Child. Concluded.

Rit. . . . . ⌢ **A tempo.**

Fa-ther of pit-y, of compassion, and love; Drinker, oh, think of
hus-band as dear as in hap-pi-er days, Cher-ish me still! make
low you have bro't us by in-dulging in drink; Bless us to-night by
save you from drink, if you'll turn to him now; *Turn from your ru - in,*

childhood and home, Cast off your fetters by giving up rum.
hap-py our home, Choose me in-stead of death-dealing rum.
giv-ing up rum, An - gels will bear the tidings back home.
turn from your rum, *List to his voice— O wan-der-er, come!*

CHORUS. *f* **Allegretto.**

1. Each hour do their pleadings and sadness but mark, To you they are pleading, O brother* now hark.

4. Each hour does his pleading, etc.   For you he is pleading, O wanderer, hark!

p **Dolce. Andante.**   **Rit.** **Repeat** *pp*

Bless us to-night by giving up rum, Angels will bear the tidings back home.

*Substitute for 2d verse, " Husband ;" for 3d verse, " Father."

No. 56.   Who's on the Lord's Side?

PAULINA.   "Who is on the Lord's side."—EX. 32: 26.   P. P. BLISS, by per.

1. We're marching to Ca-naan with ban-ner and song, We're soldiers en-
2. The sword may be burnished, the ar-mor be bright, For Sa-tan ap-

list - ed to fight 'gainst the wrong; But, lest in the con-flict our
pears as an an - gel of light; Yet dark - ly the bos-om may

strength should divide, We ask, Who a-mong us is on the Lord's side?
treach - er - y hide, While lips are professing, "I'm on the Lord's side."

CHORUS.

Oh, who is there a-mong us, the true and the tried, Who'll stand by his

col-ors—who's on the Lord's side? Oh, who is there a-mong us, the

48

Who's on the Lord's Side? Concluded.

true and the tried, Who'll stand by his col-ors—who's on the Lord's side?

3 Who is there among us yet under the rod,
   Who knows not the pardoning mercy of God?
   Oh, bring to him humbly the heart in its pride;
   Oh, haste while he's waiting and seek the Lord's side. *Cho.*

4 Oh, heed not the sorrow, the pain, and the wrong,
   For soon shall our sighing be changed into song;
   So, bearing the cross of our covenant Guide,
   We'll shout, as we triumph, "*I'm on the Lord's side!*" *Cho.*

No. 57.   Let the Children Come to Me.

"Suffer little children, and forbid them not, to come unto me."—MATT. 19: 14.

M. M. J.   MARK M. JONES, by per.

1. Let the children come to me, Said the blessed Sav-ior, In their in-no-
2. Little brown eyes sweet and clear, Ringlets bright and golden, Precious lit-tle
3. So he takes them in his arms, Hides them in his bosom; I have need of

cence and glee, And for-bid them nev-er.
hearts so dear, How the Savior loves them.   Come to me, come to me,
these he says, Thus it is I choose them.

CHORUS.

Said the blessed Savior; Let the children come to me, And forbid them never.

47

The Ninety and Nine.

P. P. Bliss, by per.

1. There were nine ty and nine that safe · ly lay In the shel-ter of the fold, But one had wandered far a · way, In the des-ert so lone and cold; A · way on the mountains wild and bare, A-way from the Shepherd's tender care; ten der care.

2 Shepherd, hast thou not here thy
    ninety and nine;
Are they not enough for thee?
But the Shepherd replied, "This one
    of mine,
Has wandered away from me;
The way may be wild and rough and
    steep,
I go to the desert to find my sheep."

3 But none of the ransomed ever knew
How deep were the waters crossed,
Nor how dark was the night the Lord
    passed through

Ere he found the sheep that was lost.
Away in the desert he heard its cry,
So feeble and helpless and ready to die.

4 And afar up the mountain, thunder
    riven,
And along the rocky steep,
There arose the glad song of joy to
    heaven,
"Rejoice, I have found my sheep!"
And the angels echoed around the
    throne,
"Rejoice, for the Lord brings back his
    own!"

Deliverance Will Come.

REV. W. McDONALD. By per.

1. { I saw a way-worn trav'ler In tat-tered garments clad, And
   { His back was lad-en hea-vy, His strength was almost gone, Yet he

2. { The sum-mer sun was shining, The sweat was on his brow, His
   { But he kept pressing onward, For he was wending home; Still

struggling up the mountain, It seemed that he was sad.)
shout-ed as he journeyed, De-liv-erance will come. } Then palms of

garments worn and dust-y, His step seemed very slow.)
shout-ing as he journeyed, De-liv-erance will come. } Then palms of

vic-to-ry, Crowns of glo-ry, Palms of vic-to-ry I shall wear.

3 The songsters in the arbor
   That grew beside the way,
   Attracted his attention,
   Inviting his delay ;
   His watchword being " Onward !"
   He stopped his ears and ran,
   Still shouting as he journeyed,
   Deliverance will come. *Cho.*

4 I saw him in the evening,
   The sun was bending low,
   Had overtopped the mountain
   And reached the vale below;
   He saw the golden city,
   His everlasting home,
   And shouted loud hosannah !
   Deliverance will come. *Cho.*

5 While gazing on that city
   Just o'er the narrow flood,
   A band of holy angels
   Came from the throne of God ;
   They bore him on their pinions,
   Safe o'er the dashing foam,
   And joined him in his triumph,—
   Deliverance has come. *Cho.*

6 I heard the song of triumph
   They sang upon that shore,
   Saying, Jesus has redeemed us,
   To suffer nevermore;
   Then casting his eyes backward,
   On the race which he had run,
   He shouted loud hosannah !
   Deliverance has come. *Cho.*

4

No. 60. We'll Work for Temp'rance Movements.

Words arr.   AIR.—*Gwine to ride, etc.*   By per. Biglow & Main.

SOLO.   **CHORUS.**

1. We will work for temp'rance* movements, The Lord's work advancing;
2. We will wear the badge of heav'n's blue, The Lord's work advancing;
3. We will raise up fall-en com-rades, The Lord's work advancing;
4. We will work for to-tal abstinence, The Lord's work advancing;

SOLO.   **CHORUS.**

Work for temp'rance movements, The Lord's work ad - vanc-ing;
Wear the badge of heav'n's blue, The Lord's work ad - vanc-ing;
Raise up fall-en com - rades, The Lord's work ad - vanc-ing;
Work for to - tal abstinence, The Lord's work ad - vanc-ing;

SOLO.   **CHORUS.**

Work for temp'rance movements, The Lord's work advancing, O - ver
Wear the badge of heav'n's blue, The Lord's work advancing, O - ver
Raise up fall-en comrades, The Lord's work advancing, O - ver
Work for to - tal abstinence, The Lord's work advancing, O - ver

CHORUS.

all our no-ble land. O com - rades, come and sign the pledge,

* The word "Reynolds" or "Murphy" may be used instead.

We'll Work for Temp'rance, etc. Concluded.

O com-rades, come and sign the pledge, O com-rades,

come and sign the pledge, And join our temp'rance band.

No. 61.   Ring the Bells of Heaven.

1 Drop a glad thanksgiving from your lips to-night,
  For the chain that fettered you is riven;
Bid the shining angels, hovering in sight,
  Carry back the joyful news to heaven.

  CHORUS.—Rise, my brother! take an upward start!
    Wear the Ribbon right above your heart;
    As we rally round you, take the pledge and sign,
    "Abstinence from Whisky, Rum, and Wine."

2 Throw the portals open—light the distant track—
  For the sheep returning from the wold,
Caught by snare and pitfall—helpless to come back,
  Shepherds found and bore them to our fold. *Cho.*

3 Join our loudest praises—triumphs should begin
  When repentant wanderers return;
Prodigals grown weary of the paths of sin
  Must be taught the tempting cup to spurn. *Cho.*
                          KATE HARRINGTON.

No. 62.   New Sweet By and By.

1 There's a hope that is richer by far
  Than jewels or gold from the mine;
'Tis the promise that, vile tho' we are,
  We may merit his pardon divine.

  CHORUS.
In the sweet by and by,
  Where sin nor its shadow may
  come,
In the sweet by and by,
  We shall meet in that beautiful
  home.

2 'Tis like Gilead's balm to the soul
  Of the wretched despised and op-
  pressed,
The thought that we bid them enroll
  Their names with the purest and
  best. *Cho.*

3 There is only one Father above,
  And all are his children below;
The gifts of his pardon and love
  Are free to the high and the low. *Cho.*
                KATE HARRINGTON.

Hold the Fort.

P. P. B.

P. P. BLISS, by per.

1. Ho! my comrades, see the sig - nal, Waving in the sky!
2. See the mighty host ad - vancing, Sa - tan lead-ing on;

Re - in-forcements now ap - pear-ing, Vic - to - ry is nigh!
Might - y men a - round us fall-ing, Cour-age a-lmost gone.

CHORUS.

"Hold the fort, for I am com-ing," Je - sus sig - nals still,

Wave the an - swer back to heaven, "By thy grace we will."

3 See the glorious banner waving,
    Hear the bugle blow;
  In our Leader's name we'll triumph
    Over every foe.
       "Hold the fort," etc.

4 Fierce and long the battle rages,
    But our help is near;
  Onward comes our Great Commander,
    Cheer, my comrades, cheer!
       "Hold the fort," etc.

No. 64. Courage.

TUNE.—*Hold the Fort.*

1 Loose the life-boat—set it bounding
   O'er the foaming wave,
   To yon wrecks of manhood trembling
   O'er a yawning grave.

CHORUS.

Grasp the shrouds, O, sinking brothers,
   Ere your footholds slip;
Courage, now, and we will bear you
   To our temperance ship.

2 Though the night be dark and starless
   Do not start nor shrink;
   Kindly hands are stretched to snatch
      you
   From the fearful brink.—CHO.

3 And, though hungry waves have
      swallowed,
   All your hoarded dross,
   If your precious souls are rescued,
   Never mourn your loss.—CHO.

4 Once aboard our noble vessel,
   Pledged to purpose true,
   We will urge, encourage, aid you,
   Till you start anew.—CHO.

KATE HARRINGTON.

No. 65. Firmly Stand.

TUNE.—*Hold the Fort.*

1 Welcome, comrades, glad we greet
      you,
   In our temperance throng;
   Now, let all, with hearts and voices,
   Raise the joyous song.

CHORUS.

Firmly stand for truth and temperance,
   Each be faithful still;
Hear the answer loudly ringing,
   By God's grace we will.

2 Men and women, youth and maidens,
   March against the foe,
   With the strength of Christ invested,
   Praying as you go.—CHO.

3 Many foes are pressing round us,
   Earth and hell unite;
   Fear them not, be true and steadfast.
   God will aid the right.—CHO.

4 Fiercely now the conflict rages,
   Long the strife may be;
   But a glorious day draws nearer—
   Day of victory!—CHO.

5 On, then, comrades, ever onward,
   No such word as fail;
   Rest not till the foe be vanquished,
   And the right prevail.—CHO.

No. 66. Take your Stand.

TUNE.—*Hold the Fort.*

1 Hear the glorious anthem swelling,
   From the hearts so true and brave;
   Many noble men are striving
   Fallen ones to save.

CHORUS.

Join the army, push the contest,
   Aid the noble band;
Till the demon rum is vanquished,
   Driven from the land.

2 Many dying victims call you,
   Lend to them a helping hand;
   From the rolling sea of anguish
   Bring them safe to land.—CHO.

3 Fierce and many great temptations
   Come to them on every hand;
   Blame not those who may have fallen,
   Help them firm to stand.—CHO.

4 Now the ranks of vice are breaking,
   They are falling thick and fast;
   Persevere a little longer,
   Vict'ry's yours at last.—CHO.

EMMA BELL.

No. 67. Come up and Sign!

TUNE.—*Tramp, Tramp, Tramp.*

1 We have gathered here to-night,
   We have dared to do the right!
   For our hearts are brave and we
      will stand the storm:
   We will drive away despair,
   And the ribbon we will wear,
   And we'll help our fallen brothers
      to reform.

CHORUS.

Come, come, come and join our order,
Come up boldly now and sign,
   Come and dare to do the right,
   It will make your pathway bright;
God will keep you with his grace
   and love divine.

2 Do not say "another time,"
   For to wait is almost crime;
   Come and show your colors boldly
      in our hall!
   All your friends will give you praise,
   And you know the Bible says
   We should love our fellow beings
      first of all.—CHO.

3 And the little children too,
   Let them come and wear the blue—
   For their little hearts are with us
      in our work;
   Let them come and take their stand,
   And throughout the beauteous land,
   Demon Alcohol no more will dare to lurk.

FRANK M. GILBERT.

55

No. 68. Sing We Merrily.

W. HOYLE.

J. MERRITTE DRIVER.

Lively.

1. Sing we mer-ri-ly, sing we mer-ri-ly, Joyful strains we hither bring;

2. Joy and happiness, joy and happiness Flow to cheer us on our way;

Sweetest har-mo-ny, sweetest harmony, Shall the waking echoes ring.

Love and puri - ty, love and puri - ty, Fill our hearts from day to day.

CHORUS.

Welcome friend and welcome stranger, All who love the soul of song;

All who love the cause of freedom, Welcome to our festive throng.

3 Homes are beautiful, homes are beautiful,
Children sing and children play;
Earth seems lovelier, earth seems lovelier,
Where true temp'rance holds her sway. *Cho.*

No. 69. Yield not to Temptation.

H. R. P.

H. R. PALMER, by per.

1. Yield not to temp-ta-tion, For yielding is sin, Each vic-t'ry will
2. Shun e - vil compan-ions, Bad language disdain, God's name hold in
3. To him that o'ercom-eth God giv-eth a crown, Thro' faith we shall

help us Some oth - er to win; Fight man - ful - ly on-ward,
rev-'rence, Nor take it in vain; Be thoughtful and ear-nest,
con-quer, Though oft-en cast down; He who is our Sav - ior

Dark passions sub-due, Look ev-er to Je - sus, He'll carry you through.
Kind hearted and true, Look ev-er to Je - sus, He'll carry you through.
Our strength will renew, Look ev-er to Je - sus, He'll carry you through.

CHORUS.

Ask the Sav- ior to help you, Com-fort, strengthen, and keep you;

He is will-ing to aid you, He will car - ry you through.

35

No. 70. Hurrah! for Sparkling Water.

-FANNY J. CROSBY.
J. MERRITTE DRIVER.

1. Hur-rah! for sparkling wa - ter, The cool, the pure and free;
2. Hur-rah! for sparkling wa - ter, We love the pearl - y rill,
3. As stream with stream u - nit - ing, In beau - ty wend their way,

The sil - ver plashing wa - ter, That murmurs o'er the lea;
That glides a - long the val - ley, Be - side the woodland hill;
To seek the might-y o - cean, And min - gle with the spray;

It gives us health and vig - or, It makes us bold and strong;
The mer - ry, laugh-ing wa - ter, We hail it with de - light;
So may our grow-ing num-bers, Our strength and u-nion prove,

Un - furl the temp'rance ban-ner, And this shall be our song.
It fills our hearts with gladness, And makes our dwelling bright.
Till all shall reach the ha - ven Of joy and peace and love.

Hurrah! for Sparkling Water. Concluded.

Hur-rah! hur-rah! hur - rah!

CHORUS.

Hur-rah! hur - rah! hur-rah! Hur-

rah! for sparkling wa - ter; Hur-rah! hur - rah! for

wa - ter, The cool, the pure and free. . . . .

No. 71. **Pardon, to-night, Mother.**

TUNE.—*Rock me to Sleep, Mother.*

1 Mother, dear mother, if friends may
    draw near,
  When souls are pardoned, I feel you
    are here,
  Hovering o'er me on pinions of white,
  Clasping the hand of your darling
    to-night;
  Tenderly pressing your lips to my brow,
  Making their baptism the seal of my vow,
  Only to find me a wreck and a blight,
  Pleading for pardon—for pardon to-
    night.

2 Was it your spirit imploring with
    mine,
  Fondly persuading, impelled me to
    sign?
  Did you glide softly in rapturous
    joy,
  Close to the heart of your penitent
    boy?

Pillow his head where so oft it had lain,
Urge him, with kisses and tears, to refrain,
Only to find him a wreck and a blight,
Pleading for pardon—for pardon to-
    night?

3 Often, when haunting the by-ways of
    sin,
  Mother, your sweet angel-voice floated
    in;
  Earnest beseeching, yet gentle its tone,
  Breathing the prayer that my child-
    hood had known:
  "Lead him not into temptation," you
    cried,
  Just as you did when I knelt by your
    side;
  Yet you have found me a wreck and
    a blight,
  Pleading for pardon—for pardon to-
    night.   KATE HARRINGTON.

No. 72. We'll Drink No More.

J. M. D. J. MERRITTE DRIVER.

Spirited.

1. We'll drink no more the beaming wine, We'll be no more its servile slave;
2. We'll use our influence, young and old, Against this e - vil of our land;
3. We'll save our brothers from the walk Which leads to ruin, woe and death;
4. We'll rescue those quite near the grave, Who've almost crossed the river deep,
5. Oh, God! in mer - cy help us keep The solemn vow we make to-night,

We'll bow no more at such a shrine, That makes a coward of the brave.
A-gainst this dread ag-gress-or bold, Who'd ruin all with ruthless hand.
We'll on the highways plead and talk, And crown abstainers with a wreath.
Now sink-ing to a drunkard's grave, While loving ones so sadly weep.
And from this start, oh, may we reap A home at last where comes no night.

CHORUS.

We'll bow no more be - fore a god That rules us
We'll bow no more be-fore a god That rules

with an i - ron rod, But drink from rills so
us with an i - ron rod, But drink from rills so

pure and bright, And sign the pledge right here to-night.
pure and bright,

No. 73.   God Speed the Right.

"And every man that striveth for the mastery is temperate in all things."

From the German.

f With spirit.

1. Now   to heav'n our prayer as - cend - ing   God speed the right!
2. Be   that prayer a - gain re - peat - ed,   God speed the right!
3. Pa - tient, firm, and per - se - ver - ing,   God speed the right!

f

In   a   no - ble cause con - tend - ing,   God speed the right!
Ne'er de - spair - ing tho' de - feat - ed,   God speed the right!
Ne'er the e - vent   our dan - ger fear - ing,   God speed the right!

Ee their zeal in heav'n re - cord - ed,   With suc - cess on
Like the good and great in   sto - ry,   If   they fall, they
Pains, nor toils, nor tri - als heed - ing,   And   in heav'n's own

ff

earth re - ward - ed.   God speed the right!
fall with glo - ry,   God speed the right!   God speed the right!
time succeeding,   God speed the right!

No. 74. Belshazzar's Feast.

B. W. Proctor.

J. Merritte Driver.

Moderato.

1. Bel-shaz-zar is king, Bel-shaz-zar is lord, And a thousand dark

1. Bel-shaz-zar is king, Bel-shaz-zar is lord, And a thousand dark

nobles all bend at his board; Fruits glisten, flow'rs blossom, meats

nobles all bend at his board; Fruits glisten, flow'rs blossom, meats steam, and a flood Of the wine that man loveth runs redder than blood; Wild

steam, and a flood Of the wine that man loveth runs redder than blood; Wild

Con Brio.

dancers are there, and a ri - ot of mirth, And the beau - ty that

dancers are there, and a ri - ot of mirth, And the beau - ty that

61

Animato.

maddens   the   pas-sions of earth ; And the crowds all shout, till the

maddens   the pas - sions of earth ; And the crowds all shout, till the

vast roofs ring—All praise to Belshaz-zar, . . Bel-shaz-zar, the king!

vast roofs ring—All praise to Belshaz-zar, . . Bel-shaz-zar, the king!

Belshazzar's Feast. Continued.

1st time. | 2d time PP

Grandioso.

2. "Bring forth," cries the monarch, "the vessels of gold Which my

2. "Bring forth," cries the monarch, "the vessels of gold Which my

65

father tore down from the temples of old; Bring forth, and we'll drink, while the

father tore down from the temples of old; Bring forth, and we'll drink, while the

trumpets are blown, To the gods of bright silver, of gold, and of stone;

trumpets are blown, To the gods of bright silver, of gold, and of stone;

Belshazzar's Feast. Continued.

Bring forth!" and be-fore him the vessels all shine, And he bows un - to

Bring forth!" and be-fore him the vessels all shine, And he bows un - to

Ba-al, and he drinks the dark wine; While the trumpets bray, and the

Ba-al, and he drinks the dark wine; While the trumpets bray, and the

5

cymbals ring,—" Praise, praise to Belshazzar, Bel-shaz - zar, the king!"

cymbals ring,—" Praise, praise to Belshazzar, Bel-shaz - zar, the king!"

Con molto Agitato.

3. Now, what com-eth!

3. Now, what com-eth!

look! look!—without menace or call? Who writes with the lightning's bright

look! look!—without menace or call? Who writes with the lightning's bright

hand on the wall? What pierceth the king like the point of a dart? What

hand on the wall? What pierceth the king like the point of a dart? What

Belshazzar's Feast. Continued.

drives the bold blood from his cheek to his heart? "Chaldeans! Magicians! the

drives the bold blood from his cheek to his heart? "Chaldeans! Magicians! the

letters expound! They are read—and Belshazzar is dead on the ground!"

letters expound! They are read—and Belshazzar is dead on the ground!"

DUET. Con express.

Belshazzar's Feast. Concluded.

Hark! The Persian is come on a con - queror's wing, And a

Hark! The Persian is come on a con - queror's wing, And a

Mede's on the throne of Bel - shaz - zar, Belshaz-zar the king.

Mede's on the throne of Bel - shaz - zar, Belshaz-zar the king.

INDEX.

Titles in Small Caps; first lines in Roman.